Destination Dad 2.0

A Fathers Journey

ILYNMW Publishing
Atlanta Georgia

DEDICATION

This book is dedicated to my Beautiful Bride and the love of my life - Debbie. In addition, I want to dedicate this book to my children - Hannah, David, Sarah and Jonathan. I am so proud of you guys and I love you no matter what!

paulbeersdorf@gmail.com

Published by: ILYNMW Publishing

v12.0

Our commitment – 100% of proceeds to Charity

Cover Design: Paul Beersdorf

ISBN 978-0-9983413-5-4

Books by Paul Beersdorf

Flowers on Tuesday

The 100 Most Important Words

Encouraging Your Wife

Encouraging Your Husband

Advice for Today, Tomorrow and Forever

Even Moses Needed Encouragement

Storm Management

Living Intentionally

Choosing to Finish Well

Luck, Chance or Prayer

Unleadership

CONTENTS

ACKNOWLEDGEMENTS

I love my Beautiful Bride and how much she encourages me to write and share my thoughts and ideas.   She is the love of my life and my best friend. Nothing I do would be worthwhile without her by my side.

To Hannah, David, Sarah Grace and Jonathan – thank you for putting up with Dad 1.0 for so many years!   Thank you for allowing me to pursue the Dad 2.0 journey.   You guys are so worth the trip!

INTRODUCTION

"The choice we face (in life) is between empty self-indulgence and meaningful activity". **Billy Graham**

I have four children – Hannah, David, Sarah Grace and Jonathan. As of this writing Hannah is 29 as the oldest and Jonathan is 18 as the youngest.

I have failed my children on multiple occasions!

I was not always the father they wanted, needed or desired.

I needed to change!

If you are reading this book, then perhaps you see the need to make changes in your life and you are seeking some advice or counsel on how to be a better father.

For the longest time I was Dad 1.0. I thought I had it figured out and it was my way or the highway.

However, through a series of tumultuous life events I came to realize I did not have it figured out and I needed to change. These life events humbled me and showed me the need to move from Dad 1.0 to Dad 2.0.

In other words this old dog needed to learn new tricks. I needed to iterate my approach to being a father. Especially since my children were moving quickly into adulthood. If I was not careful, thoughtful and humble – I ran the risk of alienating my children and creating rifts that would be very difficult to heal.

I have found that being teachable and having the ability to iterate is one of the key skills needed to succeed in life. This is true in business and it is true with my family and personal pursuits as well.

The Dad 2.0 process has led me to make a number of different and sometimes difficult changes in my approach to being a father. I realize when you see some of the changes I have made your reaction will most likely be – "well duh! That's obvious".

While it may be obvious, it is not enough to know what to do; you have to be intentional and actually make the changes. You have to be proactive and thoughtful.

To be clear – I AM NOT PERFECT! I will never be perfect. I have flaws and foibles and will forever be striving to be a better father. It is in the striving that I hope to effect positive change in my life and the lives of my children

My goal is to finish well! I know this will be a life long journey.

You will note that everything in this book is focused on what you need to do to change! Believe it or not, you can only really change one person in this life – yourself. Certainly you have influence, and can lead, guide and direct others, but you can only change yourself. Because change comes from within!

If you want to change someone else, then pray for them and ask God to change them. Spend your time, energy and effort on changing you.

I have intentionally kept this book short and simple. We live in a stressed world where time is our most precious commodity and a long and lengthy book will most likely gather dust and never be read.

I hope you find this book helpful in your own journey to be a better father.

Just remember this journey is a marathon and not a sprint and the journey will only end when you take your last breath. I will strive each day to finish well and I hope you will do the same.

WHAT NOT TO DO!

A version of this is a chapter is in my newest book "Unleadership – Bosses Behaving Badly". As I was rereading this chapter it occurred to me that many of the same leadership traits we see in Unleaders are the same ones we see in Dad 1.0. I have modified this list for the "Dad" audience. I hope you take this to heart as you read this list.

I get it! We live in a time starved society. We want the 10 second tweet and then move on to something else. So for those of you who just want me to cut to the chase, here are the top things you should never do as a father. If you want to know a bit more than this, keep reading beyond this chapter.

Top Things You Should Never Do as a Father:

1. Micromanage your children
2. Lie to your children
3. Criticize your children in public
4. Play favorites
5. Have unclear expectations
6. Fail to give or receive feedback
7. Fail to listen carefully
8. Fail to consider both sides of a story
9. Multi-task in front of your kids
10. Manipulate or bully
11. Yell or scream
12. Fail to delegate
13. Be inflexible
14. Be inconsistent
15. Be indecisive
16. Be inconsiderate
17. Be ignorant
18. Be irresponsible
19. Be arrogant
20. Be absent

21. Be disingenuous
22. Be disorganized
23. Be unrealistic
24. Be unapologetic
25. Be unfaithful
26. Be greedy with your time, talents or treasures
27. Be unaccountable
28. Don't try to live vicariously through your children
29. Don't crush their dreams
30. Don't break your promises (or don't make promises you cannot keep)

I know this is a long list, and believe me, it could have been much longer. If you are currently exhibiting these behaviors, please take the necessary steps to stop and become Dad 2.0.   I made many of these mistakes (and sometimes I still fail and make them even now), but I would implore you to take a stand and determine in your mind to become Dad 2.0.

ABIDE WITH GOD

I am the vine, you are the branches; he who abides in Me and I in him, he bears much fruit, for apart from Me you can do nothing. John 15:5

What do I mean by abide with God? It is very simple!   Spending time with God

1.   Read God's Word
2.   Meditating on God's Word
3.   Listening to praise and worship music
4.   Daily prayers & Continual prayers
5.   Attending worship services

It is not overly complicated.   Look at where you spend your time, where your spend your money and how your use your skills and abilities.

If you are focused on improving your relationship with God – all other relationships will flow from that following.   Walking closer to God will allow you to walk closer to your children and to love and cherish them just as God loves and cherishes you.

Focus on improving yourself through a closer walk with God and you will start to see the fruits of the Sprit manifest themselves in your life and you will be well on your way to becoming Dad 2.0.

Galatians 5:22-23

But the fruit of the Spirit is love, joy, peace, patience, kindness, goodness, faithfulness, 23 gentleness, self-control; against such things there is no law.

LEAD WITH HUMILITY

*"Humility is not thinking less of yourself, it is thinking of yourself less."*_C.S. Lewis

One of the deadliest traps a father can fall into is pride! A father filled with pride is not teachable, is not patient, does not tolerate imperfection and looks for the bad instead of the good. It is ironic that a father filled with pride can never truly be "proud "of his children.

I ask myself this question each day – "What would a humble man do?"

In other words, when I am confronted with a situation with my children, instead of being the dude with all the answers and solutions, I seek to think about how a humble man would approach the situation.

A humble man:

- does not seek the spot light
- listens to others
- does not have all the answers
- is not afraid to try a new approach
- is not afraid to admit he is wrong
- is not afraid to seek wise counsel and advice

What does the Bible have to say about pride?

• God is opposed to the proud	James 4:6
• God detests the proud of heart	Proverbs 16:5
• Pride brings disgrace	Proverbs 11:2
• Pride Brings Destruction	Proverbs 16:18
• Where there is strife there is pride	Proverbs 13:10
• Pride brings a person low	Proverbs 29:23
• Do not be proud	Romans 12:6
• Love is not proud	1 Corinthians 13:4

There is only one antidote to pride – that is humility. One of the best qualities a great father can have is humility.

Let's talk about tips on HUMILITY for a father:

Tips on Humility

1. The humble father is thoughtful and considerate. He never makes snap judgments about his children.

2. The humble father follows the "golden rule" – he treats his children the way he wants to be treated.

3. The humble father is a teacher and willing to give of himself so that his children can learn and have productive lives and careers.

4. The humble father is willing to talk to and learn from anyone and everyone.

5. The humble father does not pretend to have all the answers. He is not afraid to ask for help or say "I don't know".

6. The humble father takes full accountability and responsibility for himself and his family.

7. The humble father puts his children's needs, hopes and desires above his own.

8. The humble father is quick to listen and slow to anger.

9. The humble father is generous with his time, talents and treasures.

10. The humble father says "thank you" publicly and privately.

11. The humble father does not try to live vicariously through his kids.

ASK YOUR BRIDE

"House and wealth are an inheritance from fathers, But a prudent Bride is from the Lord." Proverb 19:14

If you have children, then most likely you have a Bride as well (I realize some of you may be widowers, and or divorced). The Bible tells us in Proverbs 18:22 that -" He who finds a bride finds a good thing and obtains favor from the Lord". Since the Garden of Eden, God has been bringing a Bride alongside for us to walk through this life together.

Therefore, you should lean on your Bride and ask her help, advice and prayer as you work to become Dad 2.0.

If your Bride is anything like my Bride, then you will find that she is much more in tune with the wants, needs and desires of the children. She will have insight and wisdom into the children that far exceeds your own and will help you with your blind spots if you will let her.

I know I could never, ever be an effective father and start to move towards being Dad 2.0 without my Bride Debbie. She is a rock and anchor in our family and is an incredible encourager and infinitely patient with me as I stumble, fall and make mistakes.

Start today by telling her your inner thoughts and feeling about how you want to be a better father and that you want, need and desire her help, wisdom and counsel. Ask her to pray for you as you start this journey and also ask her to hold you accountable!

Also take the time to pray with your Bride and lift your children to the Lord in prayer and thanksgiving.

You will have to humble yourself to seek out your Bride, but you will be a better man, husband and father for doing it. Make the choice to become Dad 2.0!

SEEK FIRST TO UNDERSTAND

The full statements should be – "Seek first to understand, then to be understood".

I love to read and this is a direct quote from a book by Dr. Steven Covey called "7 habits of High Effective People". It is a great book and I highly recommend you read it when you have the opportunity.

As a father, this is critically important for children of all ages, but I have found it most critical for the teenage years (and even later).

As we watch or learn about choices our children are making, many times we are quick to judge and jump to conclusions without the entire context. This leads to conflict, misunderstanding, hurt feel and broken relationships.

They key is asking lots of clarifying questions - in a non-conformational way – in other words you need to be cool, calm and collected.

Open ended questions are the best in these circumstances:

- "Can you please help me understand why you made that particular choice?"

- "Can you please tell me more about this situation"

- Wow, that was interesting; can you tell me more about that?

Our children are going to make choices and decisions that may not seem logical to us, but in their mind it makes sense. We have to remember they usually do not have the experience, wisdom or discernment that we have and we cannot expect them to always make great choices yet. That is why we have so many years to help train and teach them.

It is in the asking of questions, that we can help them see for themselves where the issues lie and then they can have that "ah ha" moment when the light goes on inside their head and they realize they could have or should have made a different choice.

This is easier said than done! As Dad 1.0, I would usually just lecture them and tell them what they had done wrong. It was definitely not "dad of the year" kind of stuff.

I have found on multiple occasions when I start to ask questions and understand their thinking and context, I almost always have a much better response and outcome.

Choose to stop and ask the questions and be intentional about how you are going to respond.

Proverbs 2:2-5

Make your ear attentive to wisdom,
Incline your heart to understanding;
For if you cry for discernment,
Lift your voice for understanding;
If you seek her as silver
And search for her as for hidden treasures;
Then you will discern the fear of the Lord
And discover the knowledge of God.

STOP, LOOK & LISTEN

We all have two ears and one mouth; therefore we should use them in that proportion. In other words, we should listen twice as much as we talk.

Fathers love to talk and hear their own voice! We like to give commands and be heard. Unfortunately, we don't always listen – especially to our children.

I remember growing up and the old folks saying – "children should be seen and not heard. " As an old person now I understand where they are coming from, but don't necessarily agree. Children have much more to offer than we give them credit for and children many times ask the simple hard questions and speak the truth.

Dad 2.0 should listen with his full body, heart and mind. When your children are speaking here is what you should do:

Stop – whatever it is you are doing

Look – you should look directly at your child – they should have your full attention

Listen – really listen and hear them. Don't think about your response, just listen to your child and focus you attention on them.

Ask Questions – if you really listen then you can ask good questions and respond.

.

How will they know they have your full attention?

- You put down your phone and or turned it off
- You put down the remote and turned off the TV
- You stopped the activity you are doing and looked at them

Kids are smarter than you give them credit for; they know when you are listening and know when you are tuning them out. Choose to be a father who really listens.

 One last thing – you are not good at multi-tasking! Nobody is!! So stop trying to convince yourself that you are good at it.

STOP FIGHTING BATTLES THAT DON'T EXIST!

"My life has been filled with terrible misfortune; most of which never happened."
Michel de Montaigne

Do you find yourself fighting battles in your mind? Worrying about a situation that may or may not even occur? Do you play our scenarios where you "know" exactly what you are going to say and do if this dire situation ever comes to fruition?

This is called worry! Worry will never add a day to your life and change any situation. Worry is one of the most unproductive things you can do in your life. It will only lead to headache, heartache and frustration.

Researchers at the University of Cincinnati found that 85% of what we worry about never happens! And even when it does happen, the vast majority of people handle the situation better than they thought they would.

When it comes to our children we tend to worry a lot! If we are honest, I bet that probably closer to 95% of stuff never happens that we worry about.

I know I have spent way too much time worrying, fretting and contemplating about situations with my children that never happened.

So how do you not worry? It is a conscience and intentional decision on your part not to worry.

Your children can read your moods and actions better than you think. They know when you are worried. Choose to stop fighting those battles in your mind. Enjoy the time you have with your children now.

As Bobby McFerrin says "Don't Worry, Be Happy"!

Even better than Bobby McFerrin, Jesus had something to say on the matter of worry and anxiety!   I have added the extra emphasis to call out the word Worry or Worried.

Matthew 6:25-34

The Cure for Anxiety

"For this reason I say to you, do not be **_worried_** *about your life, as to what you will eat or what you will drink; nor for your body, as to what you will put on. Is not life more than food, and the body more than clothing? Look at the birds of the air, that they do not sow, nor reap nor gather into barns, and yet your heavenly Father feeds them. Are you not worth much more than they?*

And who of you by being **_worried_** *can add a single hour to his life?*

And why are you **_worried_** *about clothing? Observe how the lilies of the field grow; they do not toil nor do they spin, yet I say to you that not even Solomon in all his glory clothed himself like one of these. But if God so clothes the grass of the field, which is alive today and tomorrow is thrown into the furnace, will He not much more clothe you? You of little faith!*

Do not **_worry_** *then, saying, 'What will we eat?' or 'What will we drink?' or 'What will we wear for clothing?' For the Gentiles eagerly seek all these things; for your heavenly Father knows that you need all these things.*

But seek first His kingdom and His righteousness, and all these things will be added to you.

"So do not **_worry_** *about tomorrow; for tomorrow will care for itself. Each day has enough trouble of its own.*

Therefore my friend, I would encourage you to lay down you worries and choose to live each day as it comes.   As Saint Augustine said:

"Pray as though everything depended on God. Work as though everything depended on you."

BE A DREAM MAKER

Early in our child rearing years I had a pretty steady answer for most things the kids or my Bride would ask for. It was NO.

I was really good at saying NO and I had a pretty hard heart. I was a bit of knucklehead and a tightwad, so saving money was more important than buying things or creating memories or experiences.

It was not until my oldest kids became teenagers that I got a new perspective on my role as father and leader of our family.

I wanted to create a new standard and a new attitude, so I came up with the following mantra:

"I want to be a dream maker, not a dream taker."

As a father I know I have a huge influence on my children and my words and deeds can either build up or tear down.

If you have ever watched a house being built, you will notice it takes 3-6 months to complete. However, if you have every watched a house being torn down, it can happen in an afternoon!   Destruction is always easier than creation.

So what I really started doing was focusing on the things that were on my kids agenda and "dream" list and put aside my agenda and tried to figure out how I could come alongside them and encourage them and enable them to pursue their dreams and desires.

Now, this did not mean carte blanche for them (after all we are still the parents and need to lead, guide and direct our children), but what it did mean was that instead of saying NO a lot, I started looking for ways to say YES.

Being a dream-maker means investing my time, talents and treasures.

Being a dream-maker does not always involve lots of time and money, however sometimes it will. Each family will have to determine how much to invest, but I would only ask you to consider how you balance this across all of your children and your Bride.

Also, make sure it is their dream and not yours! We have too many friends and family members who are trying to live vicariously through their children. Spending every weekend on one person's activity is not balance and it precludes you from being a dream-maker for others.

Here are some of the things we have done to be dream-makers:

- Jumping out of a perfectly good airplane - with parachutes!
- Spending a summer in China to learn the language like a native
- Having my daughter pilot a plane when she turned 15
- Singing in a musical
- Going to Mall of America with my both my daughters
- Building a tree house

To be a dream-maker, you have to spend time with your family to understand what their dreams are and which ones are real and which are just whimsy. You do not need to say yes to all of them, but try to have more yes's than no's.

One final thought. With my older kids I like to test whether or not their idea is a true dream or just whimsy.

When they come to me with an idea and it will cost money and time, I ask them if they are willing to "put skin in the game". Meaning, how much money and time are they going to invest? If they are willing to invest their own money and time, then I know it is serious.

Once I know they are serious, then I will meet them half way from a financial perspective. If a dream is going to cost $1,000, then they have to come up with $500 and I will match them with $500.

I can honestly say it is a lot more fun being a dream-maker!

Homework: – whose dream can you fulfill today? Think of one that will not cost you much money, but will require an investment of your time and talents.

I promise you will have fun with this one!

DO NOT PICK FIGHTS, AND OVERLOOK SLIGHTS

A man's discretion makes him slow to anger,
And it is his glory to overlook a transgression.
Proverbs 19:11

When you love your children, you get to know all about them. You know
their strengths and their weaknesses.   When they are young, they don't
really have opinions or strong thoughts on subjects.   However, I can
promise you as they grow older; they will start to have their own ideas,
thoughts and opinions and don't be shocked or surprised if they are
different from your own.

I taught my children the difference between a fact and an opinion.   Here
is one of the many examples I used.

> Someone might say it is cold in the room. This is an opinion,
> because others in the room may think the temperature if just fine
> or even warm.   However, if you were to say – it is 50 degrees in
> the room, then this is a fact.

Facts are easy to teach and in many cases easy to verify and demonstrate.
As fathers, it is certainly our duty and obligation to teach our children
about facts.

So many fights and disagreements can be avoided by not having
arguments about opinions.

As your children start to grow and have their own cognitive thoughts and
opinions, don't pick fights with them.   It is so easy to pick a fight and go
down rabbit trails that only lead to hurt feelings and broken relationships.

Just don't pick fights with your children.   I can promise there is no winner!

I can also promise you at some time in your life, your children are going to try to cut you down with their words and challenge you.

They will say hurtful, painful and even untrue things about you.

At times like this, you will have to remember you are supposed to be the adult in the room.   This is where it is helpful to have scripture memorized and on your heart and mind for times like these.

Here are my favorite bible verses that help me.

Proverbs 15:1

A gentle answer turns away wrath, but a harsh word stirs up anger.

James 1:19

This you know, my beloved brethren. But everyone must be quick to hear, slow to speak and slow to anger;

Proverbs 19:11

A man's discretion makes him slow to anger, and it is his glory to overlook a transgression.

Proverbs 15:18

A hot-tempered man stirs up strife, but the slow to anger calms a dispute.

It will take great self-control to not respond in an angry and hurtful way. The old saying; "Count to 10 before you respond" is so true!   I can also testify that it works.   I have saved much headache and heartache by counting to 10 (sometimes I literally count out loud).

The other thing you can do to help improve these situations is to constantly be in prayer for your children.   It is exceedingly difficult to be angry with people whom you are earnestly praying for on a continually basis.

Take the opportunity to start each day praying for your Bride (that is what I call my wife) and your children.   Pray from them throughout the day as they come to your heart and then be mindful to pray with your children in the evening.   This is true for young children and even you adult children.

I pray more seriously for my adult children now than when they were young and in my home.

I would encourage you to make a list of all the strongly held opinions you have and determine how many of them are based on actual facts.   Then take the hard step and decide which of those opinions are worth fighting over.   In other words, how many of your opinions are you willing to defend to the death of a relationship??

FOCUS ON THE INVESTMENT, NOT THE COST

Giving frees us from the familiar territory of our own needs by opening our mind to the unexplained worlds occupied by the needs of others. Barbara Bush

I was very frugal with my money when it came to my children. Said less generously, I was a tightwad! I pinched a penny until it screamed.

I grew up very poor and learned at a young age to hoard food, money and possessions. Sometimes I never knew where my next meal was coming from.

Unfortunately, this type of attitude stretched into my married life and into my life as a father.

The good news is I have now learned to focus my attention on the investment and not the cost.

This does not mean I am not prudent with my finances, it just means I look more to what will be gained with the investment in making memories than the actual "cost".

An example would be vacation time with my family. I now view this as an investment and not a cost! The time we have together making memories helps to bond us together and create that unique family time.

One of the things I do now is look for opportunities to invest in those areas of my children's lives that are significant to them. It is important to follow their agenda and not my agenda.

You have to be very intentional and thoughtful to make these types of investments. They need to become part of your DNA and second nature to you. In my younger days this was not true, but today I am looking for ways to make these investments.

There are three key areas where I have learned to focus my investment.

1. Time
2. Talents
3. Treasures

Time - is the most valuable resource we have, so we don't want to waste even a single minute. Therefore, I want to make sure I am constantly and intentionally investing time into my children

Talents - I have to be a good steward of the talents given to me and make sure I am not using them only to make a living and get myself ahead. I can and should be investing these talents into the lives of my children

Treasures – this is the easiest of the three if I am willing to be generous! Here are some great bible verses that speak to being generous.

Matthew 6:21
for where your treasure is, there your heart will be also.

Proverbs 11:24
There is one who scatters, and yet increases all the more,
And there is one who withholds what is justly due, and yet it results only in want.

Hebrews 13:5
Make sure that your character is free from the love of money, being content with what you have; for He Himself has said, "I will never desert you, nor will I ever forsake you,"

BE QUICK TO COMPLEMENT AND SLOW TO CRITICIZE

"Praise in public, criticize in private"
Vince Lombardi

It is so easy to focus on the flaws, foibles and faults of our children. We want them to be "perfect" and never make a mistake.

Unfortunately, in this striving for perfection, we rarely take time to encourage and complement our children.

You should always look for the good first!

You should always look for opportunities to encourage! You should strive to offer 5-6 times as much encouragement as criticism. For every fault you find, you should find 5-6 good things to say!

That's not just a good thing to do, but according to research in **Harvard Business Review***, the best performing business teams use this ratio of praise. If this is good enough for the business world, it is certainly good enough for our children and our bride!!

I have found I am best able to do this when I am intentionally thinking about offering praise and encouragement. It did not always come naturally to me (as I like to focus on the "areas of improvement").

My big revelation came when my oldest daughter Hannah was in college. She was away at school and I was attempting to "parent" her via text messages. I know that sounds stupid, but I did it. I thought I was being so clever and wise.

She can home and told me she dreaded getting notifications of text messages from me because they were always so discouraging.   She did not even want to turn her phone on!

It does not take a rocket scientist to figure out that was pretty stupid on my part.

I made a commitment right then and there to her that I would never do that again.   I committed to only offering encouragement and praise in my text message and notes.

Fast forward a few years and she sent me the following text:

"Good morning! I love you 2! Hope you have a great day today! Thank you for starting off my day with encouragement"

Wow!   Who says you cannot teach on old dog new tricks.

It is never too late to start encouraging your children!   You can change you critical ways and become an encouraging machine

Colossians 3:21

Fathers, do not exasperate your children, so that they will not lose heart.

* **source:** https://hbr.org/2013/03/the-ideal-praise-to-criticism

Paul Beersdorf

HOLD YOUR TONGUE

He who guards his mouth and his tongue,
Guards his soul from troubles. <u>Proverbs 21:23</u>

There is an old tale told about a man who speaks evil about others and spreads gossip and rumors in his village. One day he feels guilty and goes to the wise man in the village to ask how he can make amends.

The wise man tells him to take a feather and that evening place it on the door step of each household he had offended. In the morning, he was to retrieve all of the feathers and bring them back to the wise man.

The man went out and placed many feathers that evening and was up at first light to collect the feathers. However, when he returned to the wise man, he had no feathers in his hands. They had all blown away in the night.

The wise man told him – "just as the feathers have blown away and cannot be gathered again, so it is with misspoken words. Therefore carefully consider your words in the future before speaking"

I bet you can clearly remember the harsh words your father spoke to you and cut you to the bone. You can close your eyes and picture him there. You might even remember the smells and the sounds that were present in that movement.

How do I know this? Because every person who has had a father, has be disappointed at one time or another by the cruel and hurtful words spoken to him by their father. I for one have been on the receiving end as well as the giving end! There are words I have spoken to my children that I wish I could take back.

With the tongue men have praised God and with the same tongue ordered others to their death. Just as the tiller on a ship is small, it can direct the path of a large ship. Even so the tiny tongue can direct the path of a man.

Our children are precious to us and we should consider very carefully the words we use to address them. This is especially true if we are angry or upset. The old rule of counting to 10 before you speak is excellent (though difficult to master). Better yet is separating yourself from the situation until you have time to cool down and consider what you will say.

So how do we start to gain control of our tongue?

Proverbs gives us some useful guidance in regards to our tongue

Proverbs 13:3
The one who guards his mouth preserves his life;
The one who opens wide his lips comes to ruin.

Proverbs 29:20
Do you see a man who is hasty in his words?
There is more hope for a fool than for him.

Proverbs 17:27
He who restrains his words has knowledge,
And he who has a cool spirit is a man of understanding.

Proverbs 17:28
Even a fool, when he keeps silent, is considered wise;
When he closes his lips, he is considered prudent.

Proverbs 12:18
There is one who speaks rashly like the thrusts of a sword,
But the tongue of the wise brings healing.

Proverbs 15:1
A gentle answer turns away wrath,
But a harsh word stirs up anger.

BE TEACHABLE

One of the greatest qualities of a great leader is having a teachable/coachable attitude. The same is true for Dad 2.0 – you have to be willing to continually learn and be coachable.

Parenting is a life long journey (it does not end when your children are grown and leave home). The things that work with young children don't work or apply to teenagers and or adult children.

If you will apply yourself to being a lifelong learner, then you will have more success in all areas of your life.

Here are some suggestions:

1. Choose to be humble – a proud man cannot learn (and does not want to learn – he already knows it all)
2. Get a mentor – an older man who you respect and is wise
3. Read, Read, Read and then read some more
4. Pray without ceasing
5. Put new ideas you learn into practice
6. Be willing to iterate and make changes – not everything you try will work perfectly the first time.
7. Be intentional
8. Have a plan
9. Realize you will never reach the end of learning – there is no learning finish line. You have to choose to be life-long learner!
10. Learn to use the word YET – as in " I have not learned that YET".
11. Don't give up!

I know this all sounds like simple stuff (because it is), but it is much more difficult to be intentional and pull this off 24/7/365. It is not enough to know what to do, you have to actually do it!

Proverbs 9:9
Give instruction to a wise man and he will be still wiser, Teach a righteous man and he will increase his learning.

SPEND TIME ON WHAT MATTERS MOST

We are all blessed with the same amount of time in a day. We each have the same 24 hours. It does not matter how much wealth you have, your physical or mental abilities or even your spiritual prowess. You only get 24 hours, just like everyone else.

How we choose to spend that time is indicative of our priorities and passions.

If I was to look at your calendar in the past three to six months, what would I see? How did you choose to spend your time?

Certainly there are many things we have to do each day:

- Eat
- Sleep/rest
- Personal Hygiene
- Exercise
- Study/develop ourselves mentally and spiritually
- Work

What about the rest of your day? How are you spending that time? I would advocate we should be spending that on the things that matter most in our lives. And what is that??

Relationships! (Prioritized in this order)

1. Time with your spouse
2. Time with your children
3. Time with your extended family
4. Time with friends
5. Time with associates and others

Pouring yourself into your spouse is critically important as you build your relationship and get to know each other better. Your spouse should be your best friend and the one you want to spend the most time with.

Ultimately when the kids are grown and gone, it will just be the two of you again and you want to make sure you have spent a lifetime building each other up and encouraging each other.

My pastor said it like this:

"When it comes to spending time with your Bride, you should do the following:

- *Dialog Daily (talking and listening)*
- *Date Weekly (just the two of you)*
- *Depart Quarterly (go on a short trip without the kids)"*

Great and simple advice.

Next you will want to spend as much time as you can with your children! There is a saying that you want to spend quality time with your kids. I say that is a bunch of bologna! You don't know when quality time will come. You have to spend **quantity** time with you kids and then you will start to produce quality time.

Sometimes quality time comes in a car ride to practice or a trip to the grocery store. Sometimes it is doing yard work together or completing a project. The idea is to invite your children into your world at time when you might think of doing something by yourself.

Don't run errands without taking someone along (grab some ice cream or treat while you are out).

It might take you longer to complete some tasks, but that is ok. Your goal is to spend time and invest in those you love.

Paul Beersdorf

LOOK FOR WAYS TO SAY YES

Dads are great at saying NO! It is almost as if this is preprogrammed into our brains once our kids are born. We have the "power" and "control" and men love to be in control! Think about who controls the remotes in the family (TV, DVR, DVD Player etc.) ? I bet they are by Dad's chair.

Saying NO is easy!

Looking for ways to say YES is much more difficult.

I am not talking about being a pushover and giving your kids whatever they ask for. We still have to use good judgment and common sense. If the kids only want to eat ice cream all day long, saying YES to that would not go over well for everyone involved.

When it comes to saying NO, I found that for me much of it had to do with my own selfishness and pride. I would say NO because I was tired, bored, irritated, or had my own agenda to think about.

When I started putting my kid's desires first, it helped me to look for ways to say YES.

Here how those request are going to come to you:

"Daddy can we............."
"Daddy what do you think about going to ...."
"Daddy can I ...."

You fill in the blank with whatever request your children have. Then think about your answer and if you want to say "NO" because of selfishness on you part, then you should probably say "YES".

To put others before ourselves takes sacrifice and discipline.

KEEP YOUR PROMISES

Don't ever promise more than you can deliver, but always deliver more than you promise.
Lou Holtz

A number of years ago there was a movement called Promise Keepers. It had seven key promises for men to keep:

1. A Promise Keeper is committed to honoring Jesus Christ through worship, prayer and obedience to God's Word in the power of the Holy Spirit.
2. A Promise Keeper is committed to pursuing vital relationships with a few other men, understanding that he needs brothers to help him keep his promises.
3. A Promise Keeper is committed to practicing spiritual, moral, ethical and sexual purity.
4. A Promise Keeper is committed to building strong marriages and families through love, protection, and Biblical values.
5. A Promise Keeper is committed to supporting the mission of his church by honoring and praying for his pastor and by actively giving his time and resources.
6. A Promise Keeper is committed to reaching beyond any racial and denominational barriers to demonstrate the power of Biblical unity.
7. A Promise Keeper is committed to influencing his world, being obedient to the Great Commandment (Mark 12:30-31) and the Great Commission (Matthew 28:19-20).

These were great foundational promises that help to make us better husbands, fathers, workers, neighbors and citizens of the world. In our smaller world as fathers we need to always keep our promises to our children.

This means doing what you said you will do, when you said you would do it and doing it with a great attitude!

Here are my promises to my children

1. I promise to love you unconditionally
2. I promise to be your biggest cheerleader and encourager
3. I promise to invest my time, talent and treasures in your life
4. I promise to provide peace, protection and provision for your life
5. I promise to listen carefully, attentively and actively
6. I promise to enter your world and be a dream maker and not a dream taker
7. I promise to always have your best interests in mind

Will this always be easy to live and fulfill this mission each and every day? Of course not! I will have to be intentional and thoughtful. I will need to humble myself and be less selfish and more generous.

Paul Beersdorf

FEWER RULES

Dads love to have rules! Dads love to make rules! Dads love to make punishment for the rule breakers and rewards for rule followers. Dads love to watch and see who will keep the rule and who breaks the rules.

When I was a young father I had all kinds of rules and regulations for my family. Some were good, but many were ridiculous in hind sight. I thought having lots of rules and regulations would help me and my bride better control our children and household.

What I have found is that we don't need that many rules. Now, to be clear, you need order and structure in your house (you cannot let the inmates run the asylum). You are the parents and should be in control.

I would encourage you to model the behaviors and attitude you want your children to learn. There is an old saying – "with children, more is caught than taught". In other words, your children are watching you constantly and will learn more from your behavior.

If you want your children to be generous – they should see you model generosity

If you want your children to be truthful – they should see you telling the truth.

If you want your children to be kind – they should see you performing acts of kindness

If you want your children to be peaceful – then you should be a person of peace

If you want your children to be grateful – then you should show gratitude

If you want your children to have self-control –they should see it in you!

If you want your children to learn patience – then practice patience when they are with you and can see you. This is tough!!

Remember, Jesus kept it simple! He only had two commandments. If He had only two, why do you need so many rules??

Matthew 22:34-40

But when the Pharisees heard that Jesus had silenced the Sadducees, they gathered themselves together. One of them, a lawyer, asked Him a question, testing Him, "Teacher, which is the great commandment in the Law?" And He said to him, "'You shall love the Lord your God with all your heart, and with all your soul, and with all your mind.' This is the great and foremost commandment. The second is like it, 'You shall love your neighbor as yourself.' On these two commandments depend the whole Law and the Prophets."

GIVE MORE TRUST

Trust if a key foundation for any relationship. In the business world one of the attributes that employees want from their boss is trust. They want their boss to demonstrate trust in their skill and ability to get the job done.

The whole point of trust is that you don't micromanage! You have to give trust to get trust!

I used to have the following attitude when it came to trusting my children:

"Prove you are trustworthy and I will trust you"

There was only one problem with that attitude. I was not giving them the opportunity to prove their trustworthiness. It was a "Catch-22" situation!

What is Catch-22? It is a situation/dilemma that has contradictory regulations.

Example - You want to get a job at a company to gain experience, but they will not hire your because you have no experience.

In the case of trust, how can your children gain trust, unless you give them the opportunity to show they are trustworthy?

Obviously you will have to use your best judgment, wisdom and discernment to determine when you want to want to put your children in these situations, but I will encourage you to do it early and often.

This will be especially helpful as they enter their teenage years and are looking for autonomy and developing their maturity.

As parents we always reserve the rights to "Trust but Verify". If trust is broken, then there are obviously consequences. However, I think you will be pleasantly surprised by your children in most situations.

BE AVAILABLE

This chapter could be titled "Captain Obvious"! This is not rocket science or brain surgery. This is just simple truth.

You cannot be a positive influence in your children's lives if you are not around and available.   You have to spend quantity time with your children to develop quality time.   You never know when the quality time will hit, so you have to be around and available to experience this quality time.

Some simple truths about fathers:

- We are all busy
- We all have jobs
- We all need "alone time"
- We can all make excuses

If you get a better handle on your calendar and time, then you can be more intentional about spending time with your children. Here are some tough questions:

1. How much time do you spend on your hobbies? Golf, Fishing, Hunting, Wood Working, etc.
2. How much time do you spend watching TV?
3. How much time do you spend attending sporting events?
4. How much time do you spend at work?
5. How much time do you spend on your phone (Social Media, Surfing the Web, etc.)

If we are honest with ourselves, the answer to many of these questions is TOO MUCH TIME!!

I would encourage you and challenge you to carve out more time for your children.   You can do this by involving and including your children in many of these activities. You can also stop doing more of what you want to do and spend time on things they want to do.   Spend less time in front of screens and more time making dreams come true!

BE THE SPRITUAL LEADER

You must choose to be the spiritual leader of your family! This is a true calling of Dad 2.0 and cannot be abdicated or abandoned for any reason. You must choose to take up the mantle of spiritual leader each and every day.

How do you do this?

You lead your family in Prayer:
- You pray for them
- You pray with them
- You teach them how to pray
- You study how those in the Bible prayed

You lead your family in studying the Bible
- You start by having your own study time
- You teach your children how to read the scripture
- You read the scripture to your children
- You memorize Bible verses together

You lead your family in praise and worship:
- You take them to church
- You take them to Sunday School
- You take them to praise and worship concerts

You lead your family in serving others:
- At home
- At church
- In your neighborhood
- In your community
- Around the world on short term mission trips

You lead your family in giving and generosity:
- Tithe to the church
- Giving to missions and missionaries
- Feeding the poor
- Supporting orphans and widows

It is a daily choice to be the spiritual leader of your family. If you have not been doing this, then take a small step today and start with prayer and then start to study the Bible. You can also read a daily devotional like Oswald Chamber – My Utmost For His Highest.

The key is starting and staying committed to leading daily.

FIGHTING

Fighting can be good and productive!   There are things that Dad 2.0 needs to fight each and every day.

What do we need to fight?

- Ego
- Pride
- Greed
- Lust
- Selfishness

How do we fight these things?

- Holiness
- Humility
- Generosity
- Purity
- Service

We have to keep our **EGO** in check with **HOLINESS**.   Ego is all about our own self-importance and self-indulgence.   Holiness takes to focus off of ourselves and places it on God.   Holiness is about daily striving to live for God and abide and draw closer to Him.

We fight **PRIDE** with **HUMILITY**.   We know that God opposes the proud and honors the humble.   You have to choose to be humble.   It is a key character trait of great leaders and Dad 2.0.

We have to fight **GREED** with **GENEROSITY**. We have to generous with our Time, Talents and Treasures.   If we model this behavior with our children they will notice!

We have to fight **LUST** with **PURITY**. We have to fight the lust of our eyes, heart and mind on a daily (sometimes hourly) basis.   We strive for purity by reading and studying the Bible, worshiping God, having others hold us accountable, and putting up hedges in our live to protect ourselves and thinking about the things in Philippians 4:8,

Philippians 4:8

Finally, brothers and sisters, whatever is true, whatever is honorable, whatever is right, whatever is pure, whatever is lovely, whatever is commendable, if there is any excellence and if anything worthy of praise, think about these things.

Psalm 119:9

How can a young man keep his way pure? By keeping it according to Your word.

We have to fight **SELFISHNESS** with **SERVICE**. We have to strive to serve our family and serve others.   You should bring your children along when you are serving others.   Your children should also see you serving your Bride and other family members.

You will do battle with each of these every day! It is a never ending fight, but it is a battle worth fighting each and every day.

Finally - Put on The Armor of God:

Ephesians 6:13-17

Therefore, take up the full armor of God, so that you will be able to resist in the evil day, and having done everything, to stand firm. Stand firm therefore, having girded your loins with truth, and having put on the breastplate of righteousness, and having shod your feet with the preparation of the gospel of peace; in addition to all, taking up the shield of faith with which you will be able to extinguish all the flaming arrows of the evil one. And take the helmet of salvation, and the sword of the Spirit, which is the word of God.
.

Paul Beersdorf

WORDS TO ADD TO YOUR VOCABULARY

Be kind to one another, tender-hearted, forgiving each other, just as God in Christ also has forgiven you Ephesians 4:32

As you work along the path to becoming Dad 2.0, you may need to add some words to your vocabulary and use them quite often. These words and phrases may be unfamiliar and or uncomfortable for you, but you cannot and will not become Dad 2.0 without being able to utter these words (and mean it).

- I'm sorry
- I was wrong
- You were right
- Please forgive me
- I don't know
- Can you help me?
- I need help
- Please
- Thank you
- How can I help you?
- Great Job!
- Nicely Done!
- Keep up the good work.
- I am so proud of you
- I love you no matter what

I began this book by talking about humility and being humble. It was not a mistake that I put that chapter in the very front of the book. You cannot utter these words without humility. Go back and reread that chapter on humility and choose to commit to living a humble life.

You Bride and children will thank you!!

A CALL TO INTENTIONALITY

Our God is an intentional God! He has plans for us, just like he had plans for the Israelites who were in captivity in Babylon.   He sent this word through the prophet Jeremiah so they would know his intentionality and encourage them in their plight.

Jeremiah 29:11

For I know the plans that I have for you,' declares the Lord, 'plans for welfare and not for calamity to give you a future and a hope.

The bible calls us to live a life of intentionality and planning (while also trusting in God and having faith in Him to deliver us and meet our needs)

Ephesians 5:15-16

Therefore be careful how you walk, not as unwise men but as wise, making the most of your time, because the days are evil.

.

Proverbs 21:31

The horse is prepared for the day of battle,
But victory belongs to the Lord.

This verse in Proverbs is telling us we have an absolute responsibility to prepare for events and occasions.   What would it take to make a horse ready for battle?

A battle horse would be trained over a long period of time. It must learn to maneuver and obey the rider (whether he was using reins or not). The horse could also be taught to kick, bite, and attack.   As a real battle would draw near then a saddle, bridle and armor would be added to the horse as well.

In other words, there was a lot a preparation involved in getting a horse ready for battle. You could not just hop on any old "nag" and hope for the best. Hope is not a strategy!

At the same time God is calling us alongside Him in the battle, he also asks that we trust and know the ultimate victory is His.

Let's also consider a story in the bible that demonstrates being intentional to achieve goals and objectives:

The Wall

Nehemiah was a Jew living in captivity in Babylon and served as the cupbearer to King Artaxerxes. He had heard the walls of Jerusalem were in disrepair and the city was vulnerable.

He was so distraught that he broke down and wept. Then he went to the Lord in prayer so he could face the King and ask for permission to return to Jerusalem to repair the wall.

When Nehemiah did speak to the King, it is interesting to note that it says the Queen was with him at that time (the queen in this case was most likely Ester – the book of Nehemiah comes before the Book of Ester in the bible, but chronologically, the events in Ester happen about 30 years before this account).

The King gave his permission and Nehemiah journeyed back to Jeruselm and set about the work to repair the walls.

This was an enormous task, so how was he going to accomplish this? He needed a plan and he needed to be very intentional about the steps he took to lead the people to help complete this task.

Here is what he did:

1. He assigned people to work on the parts of the wall that were closest to where they lived. This way they would "have skin in the game" and also ensure they did a good job, because this wall would offer them and their family protection.

2. He consistently prayed to God as he confronted problems, threats and obstacles. He knew his task would be impossible without God.

3. He spoke words of encouragement when the people were fearful and needed hope and leadership.

4. When there were threats, he established half the people to work on the wall and the other half to stand with spears and offer protection.

5. He set the example and worked on the wall himself. Not only did he lead the work, he also did the work as well. It is important for leaders to lead from the front and be a positive example, especially when the people are fearful and discouraged.

6. He did not become distracted. He stayed focused on the task at hand.

Nehemiah had a plan and worked his plan. He was also flexible enough to make adjustments when needed, but stay focused on completing the wall.

Why did he want to repair the wall in the first place?

Jerusalem is the holy city of God and he wanted to make sure it would be protected and secure (this is where the Temple of God resided). In those days a wall offered safety and security from the enemies that surrounded them. The walls protected the people and also projected power and might to ward off those who might consider attacking them.

Consider the walls in our life that protect us from the world and the constant attacks that come at us. What are those walls that help us?

- The wall of Faith
- The wall of Fellowship
- The wall of Friendship
- The wall of Family

How do we keep these walls from crumbling down and deteriorating?

We must be very intentional about the maintenance and care for these walls!

To build and maintain our walls of faith, we need to study the word of God, pray, praise and worship God on a consistent basis. We need to hide Gods word in our heart, so it is easy for us to recall during those times when the enemy is at the gates.

To build and maintain the walls of fellowship, friendship, and family, we need to make time in our schedule for others and encourage them when they need a friend. We need to spend time developing and deepening those relationships – this takes time and energy and will not happen without a plan. You cannot have strong relationships without intentionally pouring into others and letting them pour into you.

When you strengthen these walls, it is very difficult for the enemy to tear them down.

Be intentional as a father and pour yourself into your children.

Things you can be intentional about:

1. Praying for your children
2. Spending time with your children
3. Investing in their financial future
4. Worshiping with your children
5. Serving others with your children
6. Taking them on errands and doing chores together

Have a plan and work your plan! Remember, it is not enough to know what to do, you have to actually do it! Having a plan and being intentional is a good start towards being intentional.

FOUNDATIONAL TRAITS OF DAD 2.0

Fruit of the Spirit

For a father to be truly effective he will need to have a foundation of traits that will become the bedrock upon which they are able to build their other leadership characteristics.

In the Bible we find these foundational characteristics for fathers in Galatians 5:22-23. They are called the "fruits of the spirit".

Here is the list of foundational traits fathers need to have:

- Love
- Joy
- Peace
- Patience
- Kindness
- Goodness
- Faithfulness
- Gentleness
- Self-Control

The first thing you should note is that each one of these traits is a choice. Nobody can force you to have these traits and certainly nobody can force you to demonstrate and exhibit these traits. The other interesting thing to note is that these words are very simple and yet they are incredibly powerful.

This is not eloquent language, but it does not have to be eloquent to be effective.

Imagine if every father demonstrated even half of these characteristics on a regular basis. What would our homes look like?

I love this long quote from Max Lucado which encapsulates how we should think of the fruits of the spirit.

Quote from Max Lucado:

"**<u>I choose love.</u>** *No occasion justifies hatred; no injustice warrants bitterness. I choose love. Today I will love God and what God loves.*

<u>I choose joy.</u> *I will invite my God to be the God of circumstance. I will refuse the temptation to be cynical… the tool of the lazy thinker. I will refuse to see people as anything less than human beings, created by God. I will refuse to see any problem as anything less than an opportunity to see God.*

<u>I choose peace.</u> *I will live forgiven. I will forgive so that I may live*

<u>I choose patience.</u> *I will overlook the inconveniences of the world. Instead of cursing the one who takes my place, I'll invite Him to do so. Rather than complain that the wait is too long, I will thank God for a moment to pray. Instead of clinching my fist at new assignments, I will face them with joy and courage.*

<u>I choose kindness.</u> *I will be kind to the poor, for they are alone. Kind to the rich, for they are afraid. And kind to the unkind, for such is how God has treated me.*

<u>I choose goodness.</u> *I will go without a dollar before I take a dishonest one. I will be overlooked before I will boast. I will confess before I will accuse. I choose goodness.*

<u>I choose faithfulness.</u> *Today I will keep my promises. My debtors will not regret their trust. My associates will not question my word. My wife will not question my love. And my children will never fear that their father will not come home.*

<u>I choose gentleness</u>. *Nothing is won by force. I choose to be gentle. If I raise my voice, may it be only in praise. If I clench my fist, may it be only in prayer. If I make a demand, may it be only of myself.*

<u>I choose self-control.</u> *I am a spiritual being. After this body is dead, my spirit will soar. I refuse to let what will rot, rule the eternal. I choose self-control. I will be drunk only by joy. I will be impassioned only by my faith. I will be influenced only by God. I will be taught only by Christ. I choose self-control.*

Love, joy, peace, patience, kindness, goodness, faithful-ness, gentleness, and self-control. To these I commit my day. If I succeed, I will give thanks. If I fail, I will seek His grace. And then, when this day is done, I will place my head on my pillow and rest."

Paul Beersdorf

LEAD WITH LOVE

"Tis better to have loved and lost than never to have loved at all."
Alfred Lord Tennyson

How does Dad 2.0 not love their family, neighbors, team and the people they work with? Jesus taught that the greatest two commandments were to Love God with our heart, soul and mind and Love your neighbor as yourself (meaning everybody else – for everybody is ultimately our neighbor).   I believe Dad 2.0 will choose a love like this.

1 Corinthians 13:4-7

Love is patient, love is kind and is not jealous; love does not brag and is not arrogant, does not act unbecomingly; it does not seek its own, is not provoked, does not take into account a wrong suffered, does not rejoice in unrighteousness, but rejoices with the truth; bears all things, believes all things, hopes all things, endures all things.

Love is one of the most powerful words in the world. No matter the language or culture, love is powerful.   In 1 Corinthians chapter 13 (often referred to as the Love Chapter) we find an excellent definition of love and how it should be applied in our lives today.   These words may have been written thousands of years ago, but they still resonate today as if they were freshly minted on an internet blog.

What does chapter 13 say about love?

You can have faith, speak eloquently, or be prophet, but without LOVE it is nothing!

You can give all of your possession away and even your very life, but without LOVE it is nothing.

You see, your attitude matters! You have to have the attitude of LOVE to make an actual impact in the world and to have any real meaning in live. Faith is good, Hope is good, but the greatest is LOVE.

Choose to love!

1 Corinthians 13:12-13

For now we see in a mirror dimly, but then face to face; now I know in part, but then I will know fully just as I also have been fully known. But now faith, hope, love, abide these three; but the greatest of these is love

Matthew 22:36-40

"Teacher, which is the great commandment in the Law?" And He said to him, "'You shall love the Lord your God with all your heart, and with all your soul, and with all your mind.' This is the great and foremost commandment. The second is like it, 'You shall love your neighbor as yourself.' On these two commandments depend the whole Law and the Prophets."

LEAD WITH JOY

"Joy is a net of love by which you can catch souls." Mother Teresa

Joy is an attitude that we choose. It cannot be thrust upon us by someone else. You can tell if someone has joy in their life just by looking at their countenance. It is impossible to hide joy. If you are joyful, the world will know.

The opposite of joy is sadness. I do not know anybody who would make the conscious decision to be sad rather than joyful and yet how many people do we know who walk around with a sad look on their face.

You can choose to be joyful and bring joy into others' lives. Joy has nothing to do with our situation as much as it has to do with our attitude and outlook on life.

I have heard it said that pure joy comes from serving others. I truly believe this. There is nothing more selfless than a volunteer helping others and bringing joy (and perhaps peace) into their lives. We take the focus off of ourselves and shine the light on others. In this setting, our situation and circumstances diminish as we focus on serving others and meeting their needs.

Think about the most joyful times in your life. They were probably when you were serving others, or perhaps when others were serving you!!

Consider the Apostle Paul, he was in prison, in chains when writing to the Philippians and yet he tells them again and again to have joy and rejoice!

Philippians 4:4

"Rejoice in the Lord always; I will say it again; Rejoice!"

Paul Beersdorf

LEAD WITH PEACE

"A people free to choose will always choose peace." Ronald Reagan

Unlike joy, peace is usually something that is more of an inward expression and attitude.   When I think of peace I think of: Calm, Quiet, Stillness, Harmony, Tranquility and Serenity.   I know when I am at peace, it is much easier for me to communicate with God and to hear from God.

Peace and tranquility.   That is what I look forward to when I come home from a hectic day of work and a long commute.   My Bride does an excellent job of knowing that our home is a refuge and a place to bring peace and tranquility.

We are by no means perfect.   There is certainly conflict and fights (we are after all a family of six people with strong opinions).   However, peace is the norm and conflict is the exception to the rule.   We teach our children about being peaceful and creating an atmosphere of peace and tranquility. It is easier said than done, but we intentionally make an effort to have a peaceful home.

That does not mean there will be a lack of conflict, trials and tribulations, but your home can be a place of peace if you work at it!

Are you a peacemaker or do you enjoy conflict?   Blessed are the peacemakers, for they shall be called the Sons of God. Matthew 5:9.

2 Thessalonians 3:16
Now may the Lord of peace Himself continually grant you peace in every circumstance. The Lord be with you all!

Paul Beersdorf

LEAD WITH PATIENCE

"He that can have patience can have what he will." **Benjamin Franklin**

How often have we jokingly said "Lord, give me patience, and give it to me right now!" While that is somewhat humorous, it is also quite true for many of us as believers today.

Patience means we are willing to trust God in His timing. Many times this means we must wait and watch – prayerfully and thoughtfully. Consider that many circumstances that are brought into your life may be there to increase your patience and build your trust in God.

I have also found that patience leads to much better decision making.

In Proverbs, it teaches that one person's story sounds good concerning a conflict, but there are always two sides to every story. Patience would tell you to be slow to pass judgment until you have heard both sides of the story.

Patience is not one of the fruits of the spirit by accident! Just like we do not give our children everything they ask for, when they ask for it. God wants to grow us and build us up.

Colossians 1:10-12

so that you will walk in a manner worthy of the Lord, to please Him in all respects, bearing fruit in every good work and increasing in the knowledge of God; strengthened with all power, according to His glorious might, for the attaining of all steadfastness and patience; joyously giving thanks to the Father, who has qualified us to share in the inheritance of the saints in Light.

What I have found in my life is that patience comes through the experiences, trials and tribulations that are placed in my path. I have to trust God enough through these difficult times and know He has my best interest in mind. God is trying to grow me, refine me and make me a better person to love and serve Him and others.

I have to choose to be patient and choose to practice this especially when my children are with me.

This is a great quality to teach our children and the will learn it the best when they see it demonstrated in our life.

LEAD WITH KINDNESS

"Kindness is the language which the deaf can hear and the blind can see." Mark Twain

Much like goodness, kindness is an action. It is not as common these days to hear someone talk about acts of kindness, but it would be a much better world if we had more kindness.

Why is kindness so hard? Because kindness is an unselfish action and kindness does not need nor does it seek publicity or attention. Many times acts of kindness are done without the receiving party even knowing who did the act.

A real father knows how to use kindness at home to draw his family together and to appreciate one another.

How do we show acts of kindness? Three ways:

Word we say – a compliment to a friend or stranger, the right words in a crisis, encouraging words to one who has suffered a loss.

Words we send – a note, tweet, Facebook message, text, email or other form of written communication. We have some many more ways today with the incredible technology at our hands to offer kind words to someone.

Things we do – from simply helping a stranger change a flat tire, to picking up your neighbor's garbage can that is knocked over by the wind. There are literally an unlimited number of things we can do each day to perform acts of kindness.

However, I would suggest that kindness should start at home! Consider how you can show kindness to your spouse, children and family before you expend your energy on strangers.

Paul Beersdorf

Kindness is something that is "caught" and not "taught". You will need to demonstrate kindness in front of your children for them to really get the lesson.

Proverbs 3:3

Do not let kindness and truth leave you; Bind them around your neck, Write them on the tablet of your heart.

Choose today to be kind. Take the time right know to show an act of kindness to your children. It will put a smile on their face and start to transform their heart.

LEAD WITH GOODNESS

"Man has two great spiritual needs. One is for forgiveness. The other is for goodness".
Billy Graham

Goodness in the context of Dad 2.0 is meeting real needs of those around them. When we are filled with Love, Joy and Peace, we will want to look for ways to meet other's needs.

What is opposite of being good? Being bad! Do we ever have to tell your children how to be bad? NO! But we are constantly pushing them to be "good". Goodness is a condition of the heart. Being good is what leads (and should lead) to acts of kindness.

Goodness is closely tied with kindness that we just read. Kindness and goodness are always inexorably linked.

Goodness is also a character quality of God. Psalm 136:1 - Give thanks to the Lord for He is Good - his love endures forever.

Dad 2.0 will choose goodness and tie it in with acts of kindness to lead their family by example.

Psalm 23:5-6

You prepare a table before me in the presence of my enemies;
You have anointed my head with oil; My cup overflows.
Surely goodness and loving kindness will follow me all the days of my life, And I will dwell in the house of the Lord forever.

Paul Beersdorf

LEAD WITH FAITHFULNESS

"God has been faithful time and again to surround me with people that sharpen me and that make me better". TobyMac

Our world is sorely lacking in faithfulness! The divorce rate is 50%, promises are not kept, and people cannot be trusted!   Faithfulness is most definitely an outward character quality that others can see. People know if you are faithful or not!

A real father has to be faithful to his bride and children. This faithfulness leads to trust and we know trust is one of the main criteria our bride and children are looking for in their father. Every day in the little things and ultimately in the big things, a real father has to be faithful.

Faithfulness is about keeping your promise and standing firmly with your family when things are going south. Faithfulness is about showing up on time and being prepared.

We also know faithfulness to a key character quality of God.

2 Timothy 2:13

If we are faithless, He remains faithful, for He cannot deny Himself.

Luke 16:10

"He who is faithful in a very little thing is faithful also in much; and he who is unrighteous in a very little thing is unrighteous also in much.

Paul Beersdorf

LEAD WITH GENTLENESS

"Gentleness is the antidote for cruelty."
Phaedrus

Proverbs 15:1 is a good illustration of how gentle words can calm a difficult situation.

Proverbs 15:1

A gentle answer turns away wrath, But a harsh word stirs up anger.

Gentleness and meekness are both used in this context (depending on your biblical translation). What I love about the word meekness is that it is one of the few words that Jesus used to describe his own character.

Meekness/Goodness does not mean weakness; it is power that is completely under control. Jesus tells us in Matthew 11:28 that he is meek/gentle and humble. If we want to have a character quality like our Lord and Savior, this is a great one to start with.

However, to fully exercise this character quality, you will have to have a great abundance of self-control. Our natural tendency is to puff ourselves up and inflate both our ego and our station in life. Meekness and Humility are necessary to combat the selfishness that pervades our very thoughts and actions if we are not careful.

Ephesians 4:1-3

Therefore I, the prisoner of the Lord, implore you to walk in a manner worthy of the calling with which you have been called, with all humility and gentleness, with patience, showing tolerance for one another in love, being diligent to preserve the unity of the Spirit in the bond of peace.

LEAD WITH SELF-CONTROL

"Industry, thrift and self-control are not sought because they create wealth, but because they create character". Calvin Coolidge

In what areas of life does a real leader need self-control?

Diet?
Exercise?
Prayer?
Discipleship?
Study?
Work?
Internet Surfing?
Social Networking?
Spending?
Saving?
Thoughts?
Speech?
Actions?

Note that I have listed the following: - Physical, Spiritual, Emotional, Financial and Relational aspects of our lives. The point being that Dad 2.0 needs self-control in **EVERY** area of their life!!

Self-control – what does that really mean? Here are some other words that might help better define self-control:

Self-Discipline
Willpower
Restraint

Self-control means being in control of your thoughts, attitude, and actions. It means controlling what can be seen by others and also controlling that which can only be seen by God.

Self-control is what keeps us from "spending money we don't have, to buy things we don't need, to impress people we don't know". This was a quote from Will Rogers.

Self-control is about putting filters on what we allow into or mind through our eyes or ears.

Self-control is about regulating what we consume on a daily basis and not giving into gluttony and self-indulgence.

Self-control is about being thoughtful of the words that will proceed from our mouth, pen, keyboard, computer, phone, tablet or any other electronic device that will ever be invented.   Most of the time this means writing a draft that NEVER gets sent.

Self-control is about having a time of study, pray, praise and worship. It is being thoughtful on how you will spend your time, talents and treasures.

Self-control is impossible in and of ourselves. It is only through the saving grace and mercy of Jesus and the Holy Spirit living inside us that allows us to have godly self-control.

When you consider all of the fruits of the spirit, it is self-control that allows us to be used by God in such a way that will bring honor and glory to Him and His kingdom.

You should imprint these verses on your heart, mind, body and soul. Make it a part of who you are and believe and know that victorious Christian living comes when we fully live out the fruits of the sprit

Titus 1:7-9

For the overseer must be above reproach as God's steward, not self-willed, not quick-tempered, not addicted to wine, not pugnacious, not fond of sordid gain, but hospitable, loving what is good, sensible, just, devout, self-controlled, holding fast the faithful word which is in accordance with the teaching, so that he will be able both to exhort in sound doctrine and to refute those who contradict.

A real father will consider their actions and attitudes and know that attitude and actions are the two things that they can control in the middle of the crisis or trial.   A real father will know they are always "on stage" and that others are always watching them.

A real father will CHOOSE to live a live guided by the foundation elements in Galatians 5:22-23.

As a reminder, here is the list of foundational traits Dad 2.0 needs to have:

- Love
- Joy
- Peace
- Patience
- Kindness
- Goodness
- Faithfulness
- Gentleness
- Self-Control

ILYNMW

ILYNMW = I Love You No Matter What.

It is something that my Bride and I have been saying to each other for our entire marriage and something we have imprinted on each of our children. My oldest son David even had this Tattooed on his arm (not my idea, but I appreciate the sentiment).

The point of this chapter is that we should always be showing our children unconditional love. When you say I love you no matter what, it literally means I love you NO MATTER WHAT!

- No matter that you say
- No matter what you do
- No matter where you are
- No matter who you are with
- No matter where you have been

Our love should be unconditional. Just like the love that God has for us!

However, that does not mean you will always like your children! There is no calling for "unconditional like". I can promise you that your children and especially your adult children are going to do things and say things that you will not like. They are going to make decisions and choices you will not like or approve of and they may even walk away from the values and traditions you have taught them.

Therefore, you do not have to like what they say or do, you do not have to like or approve of their choices or decision, but I would challenge you to choose to love them no matter what! They will ultimately have to live with the consequences of their choices and behaviors (even as it impacts those around them).

That unconditional love you choose to show them may be the only thing they will be able to come back to or hang on to when they encounter the inevitable storms of life and the world turns against them.

You need to be prepared to keep your mouth shut, your welcome mat out and your arms open wide if and when the prodigal decides to come home!

This kind of love is enduring love! It is the love that never falters or fails. It is the love through thick and thin, in good times and bad. I love the phrase – enduing love. I have that implanted on my heart now for all my children and strive to live out the constancy of the command.

1 CORINTHIANS 13

If I speak with the tongues of men and of angels, but do not have love, I have become a noisy gong or a clanging cymbal.

If I have the gift of prophecy, and know all mysteries and all knowledge; and if I have all faith, so as to remove mountains, but do not have love, I am nothing.

And if I give all my possessions to feed the poor, and if I surrender my body to be burned, but do not have love, it profits me nothing.

Love is patient, love is kind and is not jealous; love does not brag and is not arrogant,

does not act unbecomingly; it does not seek its own, is not provoked, does not take into account a wrong suffered,

does not rejoice in unrighteousness, but rejoices with the truth;

bears all things, believes all things, hopes all things, endures all things.

Love never fails; but if there are gifts of prophecy, they will be done away; if there are tongues, they will cease; if there is knowledge, it will be done away.

For we know in part and we prophesy in part;

but when the perfect comes, the partial will be done away.

When I was a child, I used to speak like a child, think like a child, reason like a child; when I became a man, I did away with childish things.

For now we see in a mirror dimly, but then face to face; now I know in part, but then I will know fully just as I also have been fully known.

But now faith, hope, love, abide these three; but the greatest of these is love.

LIFELONG LEARNING

"Anyone who stops learning is old, whether at twenty or eighty. Anyone who keeps learning stays young. The greatest thing in life is to keep your mind young." Henry Ford

If you really want to be Dad 2.0, you are going to have to commit to being a lifelong learner! There is no short cut to becoming Dad 2.0, it is a long journey and you will need lots of help and advice along the way.

Three key things you will need to do:

1. Build your real or virtual library with great parenting books
2. Attend conferences and workshops on how to be a better father and husband.
3. Find a mentor and seek wise counsel

To do all these things will require you to be humble and admit you need help and cannot accomplish this task on your own. It will also require you commit your time and money into making these investments.

Here are some authors whose books have helped me through the years. This list is not exhaustive, just a few off the top of my head as I write this chapter.

- C.S. Lewis
- James Dobson
- Steve Farrar
- Gary Smalley
- John Trent
- Andy Stanley
- John Maxwell
- Mark Batterson

- Zig Ziglar
- Johnny Hunt
- Rick Warren
- Gary Chapman
- Josh McDowell
- Oswald Chambers

Foundationally of course the best book you can read is the Bible! I have found it very helpful to have the Life Application Study Bible. It provides a lot of history and context as well as word meanings and definitions. Ultimately, you will want to dive deeper into Bible commentary books to help you dive even deeper into Gods word.

TAKING EVERY THOUGHT CAPTIVE

We are destroying arguments and all arrogance raised against the knowledge of God, and we are taking every thought captive to the obedience of Christ, **2 Corinthians 10:5**

In my journey to become Dad 2.0, I had to make a fundamental change in my thought life. I was letting too many doubts, fears, anxiety, and troubles crowd out what I should have been focusing on. As I studied the Bible, I found these verses and have committed them to memory to help me each and every day.

Philippians 4:4-8

Rejoice in the Lord always; again I will say, rejoice!

Let your gentle spirit be known to all men. The Lord is near.

Be anxious for nothing, but in everything by prayer and supplication with thanksgiving let your requests be made known to God.

And the peace of God, which surpasses all comprehension, will guard your hearts and your minds in Christ Jesus.

Finally, brethren, whatever is true, whatever is honorable, whatever is right, whatever is pure, whatever is lovely, whatever is of good repute, if there is any excellence and if anything worthy of praise, dwell on these things.

Verse 8, the final verse tells us where we should let our thoughts wander to. They should not meander about, but we should take those thoughts captive and CHOOSE to think about and dwell on those things in verse 8.

I would encourage you to make your own list of these things you should dwell upon and choose to let your thoughts go there each and every day.

Make a list for the following:

Things that are TRUE

Things that are HONORABLE

Things that are RIGHT

Things that are PURE

Things that are LOVELY

Things that are of GOOD REPUTE

Things that are EXCELLENT

Things that are worthy of PRAISE

If you will take time to make this list and concentrate on these things, then you will crowd out those negative thoughts and begin to transform your heart and mind.

Romans 12:2

And do not be conformed to this world, but be transformed by the renewing of your mind, so that you may prove what the will of God is, that which is good and acceptable and perfect.

EVERYTHING IS NOT A BATTLE

"If you love Me, you will keep My commandments." John 14:15

I want to finish with this chapter, because it is the hardest chapter – not only to get right, but to implement.   Bath yourself in humility, cover yourself in prayer and seek wise counsel as you work to be Dad 2.0.

After 30+ years of marriage and 28+ years of parenting I can honestly tell you there are only three key battles worth fighting with your children.

Really – only three!

These are the three battles worth fighting:

1. Disrespect
2. Disobedience
3. Dishonesty

That's it.

Disrespect

I can promise you that if you let your children get by with disrespecting you and your bride, it won't be long before they disrespect others in authority.   The older they get, the more fraught with danger this is as the authority figures have a greater impact on their life.

It is one thing to disrespect your elementary school teach, but a very different thing to disrespect your boss or the police.

I know I don't have to define disrespect for you – you know what it is when you see it! You can see it in the face of a child and you can certainly hear it in their tone and demeanor.

Disrespect takes many forms and you have to nip that in the bud! Do not give disrespect a foothold in your family.

Disobedience (defiance)

This is very simple. Disobedience is simply this - Not doing what you asked them to do and or doing what you asked them not to do.

Many times disobedience and disrespect go hand in hand.

Being ignored by your children is the worst - because it is both disrespectful and disobedient.

To be clear, you can make disobedience a very broad "catch all" if you are not careful. You can create so many rules and regulations in your household, the children will be crushed in their spirit.

Don't make everything a battle by creating disobedience situations!

Pick and choose very carefully your battles and whether it is a matter of opinion or something really worth fighting about. I found that most of the battles I fought in the early years were over matters of opinion (mine), vs. real moral or ethical issues.

Remember with younger children, you have to be more understanding and patient as they may not completely comprehend your instructions or directions. Before you jump to the conclusion of disobedience, seek first to determine if they actually knew what you were asking.

With teenagers and young adults, get them to repeat the instructions and acknowledge exactly what you want them to do. Then they are without excuse and there is no ambiguity about the instructions and direction.

Dishonesty

This is the easiest on one of all to recognize. Dishonesty involves the following:

- Lying

- Stealing
- Cheating

Dishonesty cannot be tolerated in any shape, form or fashion. The trick here is not to be a hypocrite!

Kids can sniff out a lie quicker than you or I can. They know when you are not truthful.

You have to choose to live a life of integrity if you expect your children to follow you. This means being honest in all areas of your life. You cannot cheat on your taxes and expect something different from your children.

I remember years ago going to the zoo with Hannah and David when they were much younger and I watched a father lie to the lady in the ticket booth about the ages of his children so he could get a discounted ticket. I know he lied because I heard him telling his oldest son to be quiet about his real age so they could get the discount.

This father sold his integrity for the savings of a few dollars and forever left the impression with his son that lying was ok.

Choose to be different, choose to finish well and pick and choose your battles carefully.

CHOOSING TO FINISH WELL

I wrote another book called – "Choosing to Finish Well". This is the introduction to that book. I hope you find this encouraging as you start your journey to be Dad 2.0.

I am more than half way through my life, and I began to wonder what I was going to do with the rest of the time I had left on this earth? This is a common question for men and women who are at the mid-point of their life. One of my mentors suggested that I read the book Half-Time by Bob Buford. Since I am a big believer in continuing education and read 20-30 books per year, I added it to my reading list.

Since I typically read 5-7 books at a time, it took a while to work this book into my rotation. When I finally did work it into my reading list, I was so glad my mentor had suggested the book.

Even though I am well past half-time, the principles taught in the book are applicable to anybody. One of the key themes of the book is moving from success to significance. In other words, how was I going to spend the last half of my life? Was I going to be completely self-indulgent and partake in all the pleasures of retirement, or was I going to look for something more significant to do with my time, talents and treasures?

The huge ask from the book was – what was that ONE THING I was going to focus on in my life? It would be easier to create a list of the 100 things I was going to do with my life than to think of that ONE THING. What was most important? What was significant? What was most valuable? What was worthy of being that ONE THING?

As I thought and prayed about the ONE THING, it occurred to me that there were seven (7) key areas of my life that I wanted to refine and define and focus on one thing for each of those areas. They would all ultimately be driven by the ONE big THING.

These seven areas of life are true for everybody and are integrally linked together. You cannot focus on only one area without having an effect on another area.   You have to be focused and dedicated to working on all seven areas of your life and ultimately defining the ONE THING for each of those areas.   When you have done this you see how closely knit together they truly are – both now and in the future.

So what are the seven areas?
- Physically – your body and how your maintain it
- Relationally – how you deal with the people in your life
- Economically – how you manage your treasures
- Mentally – how you view circumstances
- Intellectually – your capacity to learn and use knowledge
- Spiritually –your relationship with God
- Emotionally – how you react to others

As I thought about these seven key areas of my life I wanted to distill this down to one word or phrase for each area. Not only would this make it easier for me to remember, but it would also make it easier for me to share with others.   In business we would call this our "elevator speech". In other words, it can be done in about 15-30 seconds.

So here goes – I want to be:

Physically   – FIT
Relationally   – ENGAGED
Economically   - SOUND
Mentally   – POSITIVE
Intellectually   – CURIOUS
Spiritually   – GROUNDED
Emotionally   – SENSITIVE

Note the first letter of these key words spell out the acronym P.R.E.M.I.S.E. You will see this spelled out more fully in the next couple of chapters, but for now I just want you to know that I use this acronym because it is easy for me to remember and use when I share with others.

There are two other things to consider - my overall actions and attitude. My key action should be serving others and my attitude should be one of humility. These are two key pillars that will help me with my selfishness and prideful nature.

Underlying all of this is INTENTIONALITY!   This is my favorite word these days. I have determined to lead an intentional life and will do my very best to be intentional about all that I say and do.   However, I will tell you this is easier said than done! Intentionality takes hard work and persistence.

Here is a picture of what that looks like for me:

Goal: Finishing Well

SERVE OTHERS			HUMILITY
	Physically	– FIT	
	Relationally	– ENGAGED	
	Economically	– SOUND	
	Mentally	– POSITIVE	
	Intellectually	– CURIOUS	
	Spiritually	– GROUNDED	
	Emotionally	– SENSITIVE	

Intentionality

I am a visual learner, so seeing this as a picture of a house helps me to better understand and codify my goal of living a worthwhile life and finishing well!

Now, when it comes to the ultimate **ONE THING**.

For me that is going to be serving God!   All of these other things will have to be subordinate to that ultimate ONE THING.   If I am successful in focusing on achieving the singular word that defines the ONE THING for each of these seven key areas of my life, while seeking to serve others with humility, then I believe I will draw closer to God.

It is my prayer that you will find your ONE THING and focus all of your time, talents and treasures on pursuing that ONE THING.

NEXT STEPS

Well you did it; you got to the end of the book. You have covered a lot of material and perhaps you are a bit overwhelmed. Where do you begin?

It is too late to begin living as Dad 2.0? NO!! You can start today.

Here is a brief recap of what you need to do.

1. Start with humility – commit to living a humble life
2. Seek wise counsel from your Bride and others
3. Stop, Look and Listen – give your kids your time and attention
4. Be available
5. Become a lifelong learner
6. Pick and choose the battles you want to fight
7. Hold your tongue
8. Keep your Promises
9. Be a dream maker
10. Be intentional

Remember, it is not enough to know what to do (this is knowledge), you have to actually do it (this is action).

Good luck and God Speed.

FINAL THOUGHTS

First, thank you so much for taking the time to read this book. It is my prayer this has been a blessing to you and your family.

Secondly, if you have an opportunity to send me an e-mail with your thoughts, comments or suggestions, that would be very helpful.

Finally, I hope you were encouraged and strengthened by what you read.

paulbeersdorf@gmail.com

Blessings to you and your family!

Paul Beersdorf

Paul Beersdorf

13 WEEK STUDY GUIDE

I have added this 13 week study guide to help you focus on a different area of becoming Dad 2.0. You can complete this guide by yourself or you can do it with your Bride and or a small group of men. The idea is that you would focus on one area of improvement each week and hold each other accountable

Here are the areas we will cover and focus on for the 13 next weeks:

1. Prayer
2. Role Model
3. Listening
4. Generosity
5. Intentionality
6. Dream Making
7. Entering Their World
8. Promises
9. Learning
10. Praise
11. Availability
12. Disconnect
13. Recap

There will be a pre-read/study before each week to help you prepare yourself for the discussion. Please take time to do the pre-read as this will help you to contribute to the discussion and also deepen you learning and understanding.

Each week will be a different challenge and opportunity for you to become Dad 2.0. My hope and prayer is that this 13 week journey will begin the transformation process.

STUDY GUIDE WEEK 1
<u>PRAYER</u>

<u>Pre-Read</u>

- 1 Thessalonians 5:16-18
- Luke 18:1-8
- James 5:16
- Philippians 4:4-8
- Psalm 116:1-2
- Mark 11:24
- John 14:13-14
- 1 Kings Chapter 17 & 18
- 1 Chronicles 4:9-10
- 2 Chronicles chapter 20
- Jonah 2:1-2
- Nehemiah 2:4-5
- Daniel 6:10
- Matthew 6:6
- Mark 1:35

<u>Open in Prayer:</u>

Ask someone to open in pray. Here is a suggested prayer:

Father, we praise you for the opportunity to gather and focus on becoming Dad 2.0. Help us to give our full time and attention to this discussion and to be open to feedback and suggestions. Help us to bring honor and glory to your name in all that we say and do, and to be mindful that our children are always watching us. We ask for your blessing on this time and we pray this in the name of Jesus. Amen.

Paul Beersdorf

Key Questions to Discuss

What is prayer?

Why is prayer so important for a father?

Who should we be praying for each day? Why is this so important?

What should we be praying for as we pray for our children?

How often should we be praying?

When should we be praying (time of day)?

Did your father pray for you?   How did this impact you?

How do you feel about praying in front of others?

Are you familiar with "ACTS" prayer? How would you apply this?

A = Adoration of God
C = Confession to God
T = Thankfulness
S = Supplication

Application/Next Steps for the week

1. Pray for your children by name every day this week.
2. Pray with your children this week
3. Pray for yourself and ask God for the Wisdom and Discernment to become Dad 2.0
4. Memorize the Lord's Prayer – Matthew 6: 9-13

Close in Prayer

Ask someone to close the group in prayer, with special attention on the application for the coming week. Here is a suggested prayer:

Father, we are grateful and thankful for the opportunity to gather and share with each other today.   Help us to focus on the next steps this week and to apply what we have learned.   Help us to become Dad 2.0! In Jesus name we pray. Amen.

STUDY GUIDE WEEK 2
<u>ROLE MODEL</u>

<u>Pre-Read</u>

- Job – Job Chapter 1&2
- Daniel – Daniel Chapter 6
- Joseph – Genesis – Chapter 37-45

<u>Open in Prayer:</u>

Father, we praise you for the opportunity to gather and focus on becoming Dad 2.0. Help us to give our full time and attention to this discussion and to be open to feedback and suggestions. Help us to bring honor and glory to your name in all that we say and do, and to be mindful that our children are always watching us. We ask for your blessing on this time and we pray this in the name of Jesus. Amen.

<u>Follow up from last week's application</u>

What did you learn last week as you applied the lessons from the week?

What was easiest part of praying?

What was most challenging part of praying?

What would you do different?

What was the impact on you?

What was the impact on your children?

<u>Key Questions to Discuss</u>

What does it mean to be a role model?

Who was your role model growing up? What made them a role model?

Who is your role model now? Do you have a mentor?

Why is a role model so important?

How can you be in role model in the following areas?

- o   Physical fitness
- o   Relationships
- o   Economics (budgeting and money)
- o   Mental attitude
- o   Intellectual pursuits (education and learning)
- o   Spiritual Grounding
- o   Emotional Sensitivity

Which of these areas is a strength for you?

Which of these areas is a weakness for you?

Who are some of the best role models in the Bible?

Application/Next Steps for the week

Choose one new area to be a role model this week for your kids and have a plan to teach them. Look for an opportunity to serve others with your children.

Close in Prayer

Ask someone to close the group in prayer, with special attention on the application for the coming week. Here is a suggested prayer:

Father, we are grateful and thankful for the opportunity to gather and share with each other today. Help us to focus on the next steps this week and to apply what we have learned. Help us to become Dad 2.0! In Jesus name we pray. Amen.

STUDY GUIDE WEEK 3
<u>LISTENING</u>

<u>Pre-Read</u>

- James 1:19
- Proverbs 1:5
- Proverbs 12:15
- Proverbs 18:13
- Proverbs 19:27
- Proverbs 2:2
- Mark 4:24
- Acts 16:25
- Proverbs 15:31
- Matthew 11:15

<u>Open in Prayer:</u>

Father, we praise you for the opportunity to gather and focus on becoming Dad 2.0. Help us to give our full time and attention to this discussion and to be open to feedback and suggestions. Help us to bring honor and glory to your name in all that we say and do, and to be mindful that our children are always watching us. We ask for your blessing on this time and we pray this in the name of Jesus. Amen.

<u>Follow up from last week's application</u>

What did you learn last week as you applied the lessons from the week?

What was easiest part of being a role model?

What was most challenging of being a role model?

What would you do different?

What was the impact on you?

What was the impact on your children?

Key Questions to Discuss

Would your children say you are a good listener? Is yes – why? If no – why?

Why is listening so important?

Why is listening so difficult?

What distractions do you have in your life that prevents you from listening more carefully?

How can you remove those distractions or minimize them?

How would you describe active listening?

Application/Next Steps for the week

Spend time with each child this week focusing on what they are saying (without thinking of how you are going to respond). Listen carefully and ask LOTS of questions. Show them you can be an active and attentive listener.

Close in Prayer

Ask someone to close the group in prayer, with special attention on the application for the coming week. Here is a suggested prayer:

Father, we are grateful and thankful for the opportunity to gather and share with each other today. Help us to focus on the next steps this week and to apply what we have learned. Help us to become Dad 2.0! In Jesus name we pray. Amen.

STUDY GUIDE WEEK 4
<u>GENEROSITY</u>

<u>Pre-Read</u>

- LEVITICUS 25:35–37
- DEUTERONOMY 15:7–8
- PSALM 41:1–3
- LUKE 6:37–38
- MATTHEW 6:19–21
- PROVERBS 11:24–25
- PROVERBS 19:17
- LUKE 21:1–4
- 1 JOHN 3:16–18
- ACTS 20:32–35
- 2 CORINTHIANS 9:6–8
- Matthew 6:21

<u>Open in Prayer:</u>

Father, we praise you for the opportunity to gather and focus on becoming Dad 2.0. Help us to give our full time and attention to this discussion and to be open to feedback and suggestions. Help us to bring honor and glory to your name in all that we say and do, and to be mindful that our children are always watching us. We ask for your blessing on this time and we pray this in the name of Jesus. Amen.

<u>Follow up from last week's application</u>

What did you learn last week as you applied the lessons from the week?

What was easiest part of listening?

What was most challenging of listening?

What would you do different?

What was the impact on you?

What was the impact on your children?

Key Questions to Discuss

How would you define generosity?

What does generosity mean to you?

When was the last time someone was generous to you (how did you thank them)?

When was the last time you were generous?
Of the three things listed below, which is the hardest to be generous with?

- o Time
- o Talents
- o Treasures (you money and assets)

Application/Next Steps for the week

Look for ways to be generous with your time, talents and treasures with your children. Show them how to be generous.   Demonstrate this to them and for them this week.

Close in Prayer

Ask someone to close the group in prayer, with special attention on the application for the coming week. Here is a suggested prayer:

Father, we are grateful and thankful for the opportunity to gather and share with each other today. Help us to focus on the next steps this week and to apply what we have learned. Help us to become Dad 2.0! In Jesus name we pray. Amen.

STUDY GUIDE WEEK 5
INTENTIONALITY

Pre-Read

- Read book of Nehemiah
- Ephesians 5:15-17
- Psalm 139:13-16
- Proverbs 21:5
- Jeremiah 29:11

Open in Prayer:

Father, we praise you for the opportunity to gather and focus on becoming Dad 2.0. Help us to give our full time and attention to this discussion and to be open to feedback and suggestions. Help us to bring honor and glory to your name in all that we say and do, and to be mindful that our children are always watching us. We ask for your blessing on this time and we pray this in the name of Jesus. Amen.

Follow up from last week's application

What did you learn last week as you applied the lessons from the week?

What was easiest part of being generous?

What was most challenging part of being generous?

What would you do different?

What was the impact on you?

What was the impact on your children?

Key Questions to Discuss

What does it mean to be intentional?

Would you consider yourself an intentional person? Is so, how do you demonstrate intentionality?

Why is intentionality so important when it comes to our children?

What areas of life should we be intentional?

Discuss intentionality for each of these areas:

- o Physical fitness
- o Relationships
- o Economics (budgeting and money)
- o Mental attitude
- o Intellectual pursuits (education and learning)
- o Spiritual Grounding
- o Emotional Sensitivity

What prevents you from being intentional?

How do you deal with adversity and change?

Application/Next Steps for the week

Pick a new area of your life to be intentional about with your children and put your plan into action.

Close in Prayer

Ask someone to close the group in prayer, with special attention on the application for the coming week. Here is a suggested prayer:

Father, we are grateful and thankful for the opportunity to gather and share with each other today. Help us to focus on the next steps this week and to apply what we have learned. Help us to become Dad 2.0! In Jesus name we pray. Amen.

Paul Beersdorf

STUDY GUIDE WEEK 6
<u>DREAM MAKING</u>

<u>Pre-Read/Actions</u>

- Make a list of your current dreams/hopes/desires
- Phil. 4: 4–8
- Prov. 3:5-6
- Hannah (1Samuel 1:1-2, 6, 9-11,19-20)
- Hezekiah (2 Kings 20:1-6)

<u>Open in Prayer:</u>

Father, we praise you for the opportunity to gather and focus on becoming Dad 2.0. Help us to give our full time and attention to this discussion and to be open to feedback and suggestions. Help us to bring honor and glory to your name in all that we say and do, and to be mindful that our children are always watching us. We ask for your blessing on this time and we pray this in the name of Jesus. Amen.

<u>Follow up from last week's application</u>

What did you learn last week as you applied the lessons from the week?

What was easiest part of being intentional?

What was most challenging part of being intentional?

What would you do different?

What was the impact on you?

What was the impact on your children?

Key Questions to Discuss

What does it mean to be a dream maker?

What does it mean to be a dream taker?

How can you be a dream maker for your children?

Has anyone ever helped you with one of your dreams? How did that work out? How do you feel about that person now?
Where does generosity play with becoming a dream maker?

What dreams do you have for yourself?

Which is better – being a dream maker or having one of your own dreams fulfilled?   What if you could combine the two??

Application/Next Steps for the week

Discuss being a dream maker with your children today and make a plan to bring their dreams to life.   Make a list of all of their different dreams and see if you can make any of them happen this week.

Close in Prayer

Ask someone to close the group in prayer, with special attention on the application for the coming week. Here is a suggested prayer:

Father, we are grateful and thankful for the opportunity to gather and share with each other today.   Help us to focus on the next steps this week and to apply what we have learned.   Help us to become Dad 2.0! In Jesus name we pray. Amen.

STUDY GUIDE WEEK 7
ENTERING THEIR WORLD

Pre-Read/Actions

- Make a list of all the things your children enjoy doing
- Philippians 2:3-4
- Psalm 127:3-5
- Psalm 139:13-16
- 3 John 1:4
- Jeremiah 29:11
- Psalm 121:5-6
- Philippians 2:3-4
- 1 Thessalonians 5:16-18

Open in Prayer:

Father, we praise you for the opportunity to gather and focus on becoming Dad 2.0. Help us to give our full time and attention to this discussion and to be open to feedback and suggestions. Help us to bring honor and glory to your name in all that we say and do, and to be mindful that our children are always watching us. We ask for your blessing on this time and we pray this in the name of Jesus. Amen.

Follow up from last week's application

What did you learn last week as you applied the lessons from the week?

What was easiest part of being a dream maker?

What was most challenging part of being a dream maker?

What would you do different?

What was the impact on you?

What was the impact on your children?

Key Questions to Discuss

What does it mean to enter your child's world?

Does it matter what age they are to enter their world?

What do you think is most important to them?

What is most challenging to them?

What do they fear or dread?

How can you more closely be involved in activities in your child's world?

Application/Next Steps for the week

Talk to your children and closely listen to their hopes, dreams and desires. Come alongside them as they, work, play, study, eat, pray, worship and serve.

Close in Prayer

Ask someone to close the group in prayer, with special attention on the application for the coming week. Here is a suggested prayer:

Father, we are grateful and thankful for the opportunity to gather and share with each other today. Help us to focus on the next steps this week and to apply what we have learned. Help us to become Dad 2.0! In Jesus name we pray. Amen.

STUDY GUIDE WEEK 8
PROMISES

Pre-Read/Actions

- John 16:33
- Matthew 28:20
- Isaiah 41:10
- Genesis 28:15
- Joshua 1:9
- 1 Samuel 16:1
- Isaiah 40:31
- Jeremiah 29:11
- Romans 8:28
- Romans 8:38-39

Open in Prayer:

Father, we praise you for the opportunity to gather and focus on becoming Dad 2.0. Help us to give our full time and attention to this discussion and to be open to feedback and suggestions. Help us to bring honor and glory to your name in all that we say and do, and to be mindful that our children are always watching us. We ask for your blessing on this time and we pray this in the name of Jesus. Amen.

Follow up from last week's application

What did you learn last week as you applied the lessons from the week?

What was easiest part of entering their world?

What was most challenging part of entering their world?

What would you do different?

What was the impact on you?

What was the impact on your children?

Key Questions to Discuss

What is a promise?

Why are promises so important to keep?

Has anyone ever broken their promise to you? How did that make you feel?

What is a promise someone kept even though it might have been hard? How did that make you feel?

What are the consequences of making promises we know we cannot keep?

Does it matter how old or young your children are when you make a promise to them?

What promises does God make to us in the Bible?

Application/Next Steps for the week

Make a list of promise you want to make and keep with your children. Share that with them and even consider posting it somewhere where it is a constant reminder (like the refrigerator).

Close in Prayer

Ask someone to close the group in prayer, with special attention on the application for the coming week. Here is a suggested prayer:

Father, we are grateful and thankful for the opportunity to gather and share with each other today. Help us to focus on the next steps this week and to apply what we have learned. Help us to become Dad 2.0! In Jesus name we pray. Amen.

STUDY GUIDE WEEK 9
<u>LEARNING</u>

<u>Pre-Read/Actions</u>

- Make a list of the reasons you do or do not like learning
- Proverbs 1:5
- Proverbs 18:15
- Proverbs 9:9
- 2 Timothy 3:16-17
- Proverbs 22:6
- Proverbs 10:17
- James 1:5
- Philippians 4:9
- Psalm 25:4
- Psalm 25:5

<u>Open in Prayer:</u>

Father, we praise you for the opportunity to gather and focus on becoming Dad 2.0. Help us to give our full time and attention to this discussion and to be open to feedback and suggestions. Help us to bring honor and glory to your name in all that we say and do, and to be mindful that our children are always watching us. We ask for your blessing on this time and we pray this in the name of Jesus. Amen.

<u>Follow up from last week's application</u>

What did you learn last week as you applied the lessons from the week?

What was easiest part of keeping your promises?

What was most challenging part of keeping your promises?

What would you do different?

What was the impact on you?

What was the impact on your children?

Key Questions to Discuss

Why is learning and continuing education so important as a father?

When is it a good time to start learning?

When should we stop learning and growing?

What does "attitude" have to do with the ability to learning?

What kind of learner are you?

- o Visual
- o Hand On
- o Listen to someone tell you

What areas of your life do you need to focus on and learn more about?

- o Physical fitness
- o Relationships
- o Economics (budgeting and money)
- o Mental attitude
- o Intellectual pursuits (education and learning)
- o Spiritual Grounding
- o Emotional Sensitivity

Application/Next Steps for the week

Choose an area of your life to focus upon and create an intentional learning plan and start it this week!

Paul Beersdorf

Close in Prayer

Ask someone to close the group in prayer, with special attention on the application for the coming week. Here is a suggested prayer:

Father, we are grateful and thankful for the opportunity to gather and share with each other today.   Help us to focus on the next steps this week and to apply what we have learned.   Help us to become Dad 2.0! In Jesus name we pray. Amen.

STUDY GUIDE WEEK 10 PRAISE/ENCOURAGEMENT

Pre-Read/Actions

- Hebrews 10:24-25
- 1 Thessalonians 5:11
- Hebrews 3:13
- Joshua 1:9
- 1 Thessalonians 5:11
- Proverbs 11:25
- Psalm 150:1-6

Open in Prayer:

Father, we praise you for the opportunity to gather and focus on becoming Dad 2.0. Help us to give our full time and attention to this discussion and to be open to feedback and suggestions. Help us to bring honor and glory to your name in all that we say and do, and to be mindful that our children are always watching us. We ask for your blessing on this time and we pray this in the name of Jesus. Amen.

Follow up from last week's application

What did you learn last week as you applied the lessons from the week?

What was easiest part of learning something new and being a continual learner?

What was most challenging part of learning something new and being a continual learner?

What would you do different?

What was the impact on you?

What was the impact on your children?

Key Questions to Discuss

What is praise? What is encouragement?

What is the opposite of praise?

Why is public praise so important?

Why is private praise also important?

What is false praise and how can that be hurtful?

How are we called to praise God?

When was the last time you received praise from someone? How did it make you feel?

When was the last time you offered praise to someone? How did that make you feel?

Application/Next Steps for the week

Look for ways to praise your children in each of these areas this week (if age appropriate – I realize a very you child might not have much financial acumen yet).

- o Physical fitness
- o Relationships
- o Economics (budgeting and money)
- o Mental attitude
- o Intellectual pursuits (education and learning)
- o Spiritual Grounding
- o Emotional Sensitivity

<u>Close in Prayer</u>

Ask someone to close the group in prayer, with special attention on the application for the coming week. Here is a suggested prayer:

Father, we are grateful and thankful for the opportunity to gather and share with each other today. Help us to focus on the next steps this week and to apply what we have learned. Help us to become Dad 2.0! In Jesus name we pray. Amen.

STUDY GUIDE WEEK 11
AVAILABILITY

Pre-Read/Actions

- Look at your calendar for the next 30 days and determine your availability to your children
- Isaiah 6:8
- Mark 1:17-18
- Gen. 12:1-9
- Matt. 4:18-22
- Luke 1:26-38
- Acts 6:1-8
- Luke 10:30-37

Open in Prayer:

Father, we praise you for the opportunity to gather and focus on becoming Dad 2.0. Help us to give our full time and attention to this discussion and to be open to feedback and suggestions. Help us to bring honor and glory to your name in all that we say and do, and to be mindful that our children are always watching us. We ask for your blessing on this time and we pray this in the name of Jesus. Amen.

Follow up from last week's application

What did you learn last week as you applied the lessons from the week?

What was easiest part of praise?

What was most challenging part of praise?

What would you do different?

What was the impact on you?

What was the impact on your children?

Key Questions to Discuss

What does it mean to be accessible and available to your children?

Why is this so difficult at times?

What are the barriers or obstacles that prevent you from being available?

Why is being available and accessible so important for your children?

How do you feel when others are not available and accessible to you?

How can you share more of your time with your kids? Be creative and brainstorm this! Think about where you are currently spending a lot of time and figure out a way brink your kids along.

Application/Next Steps for the week

Be intentional this week and look at your calendar and your children's calendar and determine how you can be available and accessible as much as possible. Choose to combine entering their world, with dream making and intentionality as well as generosity and I am positive you will figure out a way to squeeze more time with your children.

Close in Prayer

Ask someone to close the group in prayer, with special attention on the application for the coming week. Here is a suggested prayer:

Father, we are grateful and thankful for the opportunity to gather and share with each other today. Help us to focus on the next steps this week and to apply what we have learned. Help us to become Dad 2.0! In Jesus name we pray. Amen.

Paul Beersdorf

STUDY GUIDE WEEK 12
DISCONNECT

Pre-Read/Actions

- Make a list of all the things you have planned, and determine where you can disconnect. Make a plan to disconnect and stick to it.
- Colossians 3:2
- Proverbs 4:25
- Matthew 6:24
- Philippians 4:13
- Psalm 127:3-5
- 1 Corinthians 13:4-8
- Ephesians 6:4
- Proverbs 22:6
- Joshua 24:15
- Deuteronomy 6:6-7
- Proverbs 6:20
- Proverbs 1:8
- John 15:12-17

Open in Prayer:

Father, we praise you for the opportunity to gather and focus on becoming Dad 2.0. Help us to give our full time and attention to this discussion and to be open to feedback and suggestions. Help us to bring honor and glory to your name in all that we say and do, and to be mindful that our children are always watching us. We ask for your blessing on this time and we pray this in the name of Jesus. Amen.

Follow up from last week's application

What did you learn last week as you applied the lessons from the week?

What was easiest part of being available?

What was most challenging part of being available?

What would you do different?

What was the impact on you?

What was the impact on your children?

Key Questions to Discuss

What does it mean to disconnect?

What prevents you from disconnecting and focusing on your children?

What are the dangers of these distractions?

What signal does it send to your children when you are constantly connected?

Which of these areas are the most difficult to disconnect from and why?

- Work
- Hobbies
- Cell phone
- Internet
- Sports
- Exercise
- Ministry
- Serving others

Application/Next Steps for the week

Disconnect from your biggest distraction for a day/evening and choose to spend that time with your children.

Close in Prayer

Ask someone to close the group in prayer, with special attention on the application for the coming week. Here is a suggested prayer:

Father, we are grateful and thankful for the opportunity to gather and share with each other today.   Help us to focus on the next steps this week and to apply what we have learned.   Help us to become Dad 2.0! In Jesus name we pray. Amen.

STUDY GUIDE WEEK 13
RECAP

Open in Prayer:

Father, we praise you for the opportunity to gather and focus on becoming Dad 2.0. Help us to give our full time and attention to this discussion and to be open to feedback and suggestions. Help us to bring honor and glory to your name in all that we say and do, and to be mindful that our children are always watching us. We ask for your blessing on this time and we pray this in the name of Jesus. Amen.

Follow up from last week's application

What did you learn last week as you applied the lessons from the week?

What was easiest part of disconnecting?

What was most challenging part of disconnecting?

What would you do different?

What was the impact on you?

What was the impact on your children?

Recap

Congratulations! Here are the areas you covered during the past 12 next weeks:

1. Prayer
2. Role Model
3. Listening
4. Generosity
5. Intentionality

6. Dream Making
7. Entering Their World
8. Promises
9. Learning
10. Praise
11. Availability
12. Disconnect

My hope and prayer is that you have been blessed by this journey and are now well on your way to becoming Dad 2.0.   Remember, this is a marathon that will require you to focus each and every day for the rest of your life.   They journey never ends until we reach the end. Good luck and God bless.

Application/Next Steps

Continue to be intentional about all of these areas and have a plan and work your plan to become Dad 2.0.   I know you can do it!

Close in Prayer

Ask someone to close the group in prayer, with special attention on the application for the coming week. Here is a suggested prayer:

Father, we are grateful and thankful for the opportunity to gather and share with each other today.   Help us to focus on the next steps this week and to apply what we have learned.   Help us

www.ingramcontent.com/pod-product-compliance
Lightning Source LLC
Chambersburg PA
CBHW070814050426
42452CB00011B/2037